NARWHAL
Gratitude Journal
for Kids!

A Writing Prompt Notebook for Daily Happiness

100 Days

D0359491

THIS BOOK BELONGS TO...

_____

Date: _____

Today I am grateful for...

_____
_____
_____
_____
_____
_____
_____

My favorite thing that happened today:

_____
_____
_____
_____
_____
_____

Today, I feel...

Date: _____

Today I am grateful for...

_____
_____
_____
_____
_____
_____
_____

My favorite thing that happened today:

_____
_____
_____
_____
_____
_____

Today, I feel...

Date: _____

Today I am grateful for...

_____
_____
_____
_____
_____
_____
_____

My favorite thing that happened today:

_____
_____
_____
_____
_____
_____
_____

Today, I feel...

Date: _____

Today I am grateful for...

_____
_____
_____
_____
_____
_____
_____
_____

My favorite thing that happened today:

_____
_____
_____
_____
_____
_____

Today, I feel...

Date: _____

Today I am grateful for...

_____
_____
_____
_____
_____
_____
_____

My favorite thing that happened today:

_____
_____
_____
_____
_____
_____

Today, I feel...   😎 🙂 😐 🙁 ☹️

Date: _____

Today I am grateful for...

_____
_____
_____
_____
_____
_____
_____

My favorite thing that happened today:

_____
_____
_____
_____
_____

Today, I feel...

Date: _____

Today I am grateful for...

_____

_____

_____

_____

_____

_____

_____

My favorite thing that happened today:

_____

_____

_____

_____

_____

_____

Today, I feel...

Date: _____

Today I am grateful for...

_____

_____

_____

_____

_____

_____

_____

My favorite thing that happened today:

_____

_____

_____

_____

_____

Today, I feel...

Date: _____

Today I am grateful for...

_____
_____
_____
_____
_____
_____
_____
_____

My favorite thing that happened today:

_____
_____
_____
_____
_____
_____
_____

Today, I feel...

Date: _____

Today I am grateful for...

_____
_____
_____
_____
_____
_____
_____

My favorite thing that happened today:

_____
_____
_____
_____
_____
_____

Today, I feel...

Date: _____

Today I am grateful for...

_____
_____
_____
_____
_____
_____
_____

My favorite thing that happened today:

_____
_____
_____
_____
_____
_____

Today, I feel...

Date: _____

Today I am grateful for...

_____
_____
_____
_____
_____
_____
_____

My favorite thing that happened today:

_____
_____
_____
_____
_____
_____

Today, I feel...

Date: _____

Today I am grateful for...

_____
_____
_____
_____
_____
_____
_____
_____

My favorite thing that happened today:

_____
_____
_____
_____
_____
_____
_____

Today, I feel...

Date: _____

Today I am grateful for...

_____
_____
_____
_____
_____
_____
_____

My favorite thing that happened today:

_____
_____
_____
_____
_____
_____

Today, I feel...

Date: _____

Today I am grateful for...

_____

_____

_____

_____

_____

_____

_____

My favorite thing that happened today:

_____

_____

_____

_____

_____

_____

Today, I feel...

Date: _____

Today I am grateful for...

_____
_____
_____
_____
_____
_____
_____

My favorite thing that happened today:

_____
_____
_____
_____
_____
_____

Today, I feel...

Date: _____

Today I am grateful for...

_____

_____

_____

_____

_____

_____

_____

My favorite thing that happened today:

_____

_____

_____

_____

_____

_____

Today, I feel...

Date: _____

Today I am grateful for...

_____
_____
_____
_____
_____
_____
_____
_____

My favorite thing that happened today:

_____
_____
_____
_____
_____
_____
_____

Today, I feel...

Date: _____

Today I am grateful for...

_____
_____
_____
_____
_____
_____
_____

My favorite thing that happened today:

_____
_____
_____
_____
_____
_____
_____

Today, I feel...

Date: _____

Today I am grateful for...

_____
_____
_____
_____
_____
_____
_____
_____

My favorite thing that happened today:

_____
_____
_____
_____
_____
_____

Today, I feel...

Date: _____

Today I am grateful for...

_____
_____
_____
_____
_____
_____
_____
_____

My favorite thing that happened today:

_____
_____
_____
_____
_____
_____
_____

Today, I feel...

Date: _____

Today I am grateful for...

_____
_____
_____
_____
_____
_____
_____

My favorite thing that happened today:

_____
_____
_____
_____
_____
_____

Today, I feel...

Date: _____

Today I am grateful for...

_____
_____
_____
_____
_____
_____
_____

My favorite thing that happened today:

_____
_____
_____
_____
_____
_____
_____

Today, I feel...

Date: _____

Today I am grateful for...

_____
_____
_____
_____
_____
_____
_____
_____

My favorite thing that happened today:

_____
_____
_____
_____
_____
_____

Today, I feel...

Date: _____

Today I am grateful for...

_____

_____

_____

_____

_____

_____

_____

_____

My favorite thing that happened today:

_____

_____

_____

_____

_____

_____

_____

Today, I feel...

Date: _____

Today I am grateful for...

_____
_____
_____
_____
_____
_____
_____

My favorite thing that happened today:

_____
_____
_____
_____
_____
_____
_____

Today, I feel...

Date: _____

Today I am grateful for...

_____

_____

_____

_____

_____

_____

_____

My favorite thing that happened today:

_____

_____

_____

_____

_____

_____

Today, I feel...

Date: _____

Today I am grateful for...

_____
_____
_____
_____
_____
_____
_____

My favorite thing that happened today:

_____
_____
_____
_____
_____
_____

Today, I feel...

Date: _____

Today I am grateful for...

_____
_____
_____
_____
_____
_____
_____
_____

My favorite thing that happened today:

_____
_____
_____
_____
_____
_____
_____

Today, I feel...

Date: _____

Today I am grateful for...

_____
_____
_____
_____
_____
_____
_____

My favorite thing that happened today:

_____
_____
_____
_____
_____
_____

Today, I feel...

Date: _____

Today I am grateful for...

_____

_____

_____

_____

_____

_____

_____

_____

My favorite thing that happened today:

_____

_____

_____

_____

_____

_____

_____

Today, I feel...

Date: _____

Today I am grateful for...

_____
_____
_____
_____
_____
_____
_____
_____

My favorite thing that happened today:

_____
_____
_____
_____
_____
_____

Today, I feel...

Date: _____

Today I am grateful for...

_____

_____

_____

_____

_____

_____

_____

_____

My favorite thing that happened today:

_____

_____

_____

_____

_____

_____

_____

Today, I feel...

Date: _____

Today I am grateful for...

_____
_____
_____
_____
_____
_____
_____
_____

My favorite thing that happened today:

_____
_____
_____
_____
_____
_____

Today, I feel...

Date: _____

Today I am grateful for...

_____
_____
_____
_____
_____
_____
_____
_____

My favorite thing that happened today:

_____
_____
_____
_____
_____
_____
_____

Today, I feel...

Date: _____

Today I am grateful for...

_____
_____
_____
_____
_____
_____
_____

My favorite thing that happened today:

_____
_____
_____
_____
_____

Today, I feel...

Date: _____

Today I am grateful for...

_____
_____
_____
_____
_____
_____
_____

My favorite thing that happened today:

_____
_____
_____
_____
_____
_____

Today, I feel...

Date: _____

Today I am grateful for...

_____
_____
_____
_____
_____
_____
_____

My favorite thing that happened today:

_____
_____
_____
_____
_____
_____
_____

Today, I feel...

Date: _____

Today I am grateful for...

_____

_____

_____

_____

_____

_____

_____

My favorite thing that happened today:

_____

_____

_____

_____

_____

_____

Today, I feel...

Date: _____

Today I am grateful for...

_____
_____
_____
_____
_____
_____
_____

My favorite thing that happened today:

_____
_____
_____
_____
_____
_____

Today, I feel...

Date: _____

Today I am grateful for...

_____
_____
_____
_____
_____
_____
_____
_____

My favorite thing that happened today:

_____
_____
_____
_____
_____
_____
_____

Today, I feel...

Date: _____

Today I am grateful for...

_____

_____

_____

_____

_____

_____

_____

My favorite thing that happened today:

_____

_____

_____

_____

_____

_____

Today, I feel...

Date: _____

Today I am grateful for...

_____
_____
_____
_____
_____
_____
_____
_____

My favorite thing that happened today:

_____
_____
_____
_____
_____
_____
_____

Today, I feel...

Date: _____

Today I am grateful for...

_____
_____
_____
_____
_____
_____
_____
_____

My favorite thing that happened today:

_____
_____
_____
_____
_____
_____
_____

Today, I feel...

Date: _____

Today I am grateful for...

_____
_____
_____
_____
_____
_____
_____
_____

My favorite thing that happened today:

_____
_____
_____
_____
_____
_____
_____

Today, I feel...

Date: _____

Today I am grateful for...

_____
_____
_____
_____
_____
_____
_____

My favorite thing that happened today:

_____
_____
_____
_____
_____
_____

Today, I feel...

Date: _____

Today I am grateful for...

_____
_____
_____
_____
_____
_____
_____

My favorite thing that happened today:

_____
_____
_____
_____
_____
_____
_____

Today, I feel...

Date: _____

Today I am grateful for...

_____

_____

_____

_____

_____

_____

_____

My favorite thing that happened today:

_____

_____

_____

_____

_____

_____

Today, I feel...

Date: _____

Today I am grateful for...

_____
_____
_____
_____
_____
_____
_____

My favorite thing that happened today:

_____
_____
_____
_____
_____
_____

Today, I feel...

Date: _____

Today I am grateful for...

_____

_____

_____

_____

_____

_____

_____

My favorite thing that happened today:

_____

_____

_____

_____

_____

Today, I feel...

Date: _____

Today I am grateful for...

_____

_____

_____

_____

_____

_____

_____

My favorite thing that happened today:

_____

_____

_____

_____

_____

_____

Today, I feel...

Date: _____

Today I am grateful for...

_____
_____
_____
_____
_____
_____
_____
_____

My favorite thing that happened today:

_____
_____
_____
_____
_____
_____
_____

Today, I feel...

Date: _____

Today I am grateful for...

_____

_____

_____

_____

_____

_____

_____

_____

My favorite thing that happened today:

_____

_____

_____

_____

_____

_____

Today, I feel...

Date: _____

Today I am grateful for...

_____
_____
_____
_____
_____
_____
_____

My favorite thing that happened today:

_____
_____
_____
_____
_____
_____

Today, I feel...

Date: _____

Today I am grateful for...

_____
_____
_____
_____
_____
_____
_____

My favorite thing that happened today:

_____
_____
_____
_____
_____
_____

Today, I feel...

Date: _____

Today I am grateful for...

_____

_____

_____

_____

_____

_____

_____

_____

My favorite thing that happened today:

_____

_____

_____

_____

_____

_____

_____

Today, I feel...

Date: _____

Today I am grateful for...

_____

_____

_____

_____

_____

_____

_____

My favorite thing that happened today:

_____

_____

_____

_____

_____

_____

Today, I feel...

Date: _____

Today I am grateful for...

_____
_____
_____
_____
_____
_____
_____

My favorite thing that happened today:

_____
_____
_____
_____
_____
_____

Today, I feel...

Date: _____

Today I am grateful for...

_____
_____
_____
_____
_____
_____
_____

My favorite thing that happened today:

_____
_____
_____
_____
_____
_____

Today, I feel...

Date: _____

Today I am grateful for...

_____
_____
_____
_____
_____
_____
_____
_____

My favorite thing that happened today:

_____
_____
_____
_____
_____
_____

Today, I feel...

Date: _____

Today I am grateful for...

_____
_____
_____
_____
_____
_____
_____

My favorite thing that happened today:

_____
_____
_____
_____
_____
_____

Today, I feel...

Date: _____

Today I am grateful for...

_____

_____

_____

_____

_____

_____

_____

_____

My favorite thing that happened today:

_____

_____

_____

_____

_____

_____

_____

Today, I feel...

Date: _____

Today I am grateful for...

_____
_____
_____
_____
_____
_____
_____
_____

My favorite thing that happened today:

_____
_____
_____
_____
_____
_____
_____

Today, I feel...

Date: _____

Today I am grateful for...

_____
_____
_____
_____
_____
_____
_____
_____

My favorite thing that happened today:

_____
_____
_____
_____
_____
_____

Today, I feel...

Date: _____

Today I am grateful for...

_____

_____

_____

_____

_____

_____

_____

My favorite thing that happened today:

_____

_____

_____

_____

_____

_____

Today, I feel...

Date: _____

Today I am grateful for...

_____

_____

_____

_____

_____

_____

_____

My favorite thing that happened today:

_____

_____

_____

_____

_____

_____

Today, I feel...

Date: _____

Today I am grateful for...

_____
_____
_____
_____
_____
_____
_____

My favorite thing that happened today:

_____
_____
_____
_____
_____
_____

Today, I feel...

Date: _____

Today I am grateful for...

_____
_____
_____
_____
_____
_____
_____
_____

My favorite thing that happened today:

_____
_____
_____
_____
_____
_____
_____

Today, I feel...

Date: _____

Today I am grateful for...

_____
_____
_____
_____
_____
_____
_____

My favorite thing that happened today:

_____
_____
_____
_____
_____
_____

Today, I feel...

Date: _____

Today I am grateful for...

_____
_____
_____
_____
_____
_____
_____

My favorite thing that happened today:

_____
_____
_____
_____
_____
_____

Today, I feel...

Date: _____

Today I am grateful for...

_____
_____
_____
_____
_____
_____
_____

My favorite thing that happened today:

_____
_____
_____
_____
_____
_____

Today, I feel...

Date: _____

Today I am grateful for...

_____
_____
_____
_____
_____
_____
_____
_____

My favorite thing that happened today:

_____
_____
_____
_____
_____
_____
_____

Today, I feel...

Date: _____

Today I am grateful for...

_____

_____

_____

_____

_____

_____

_____

My favorite thing that happened today:

_____

_____

_____

_____

_____

_____

Today, I feel...

Date: _____

Today I am grateful for...

_____
_____
_____
_____
_____
_____
_____
_____

My favorite thing that happened today:

_____
_____
_____
_____
_____
_____
_____

Today, I feel...

Date: _____

Today I am grateful for...

_____
_____
_____
_____
_____
_____
_____

My favorite thing that happened today:

_____
_____
_____
_____
_____
_____

Today, I feel...

Date: _____

Today I am grateful for...

_____

_____

_____

_____

_____

_____

_____

_____

My favorite thing that happened today:

_____

_____

_____

_____

_____

_____

_____

_____

Today, I feel...

Date: _____

Today I am grateful for...

_____
_____
_____
_____
_____
_____
_____

My favorite thing that happened today:

_____
_____
_____
_____
_____
_____

Today, I feel...

Date: _____

Today I am grateful for...

_____
_____
_____
_____
_____
_____
_____
_____

My favorite thing that happened today:

_____
_____
_____
_____
_____
_____

Today, I feel...

Date: _____

Today I am grateful for...

_____

_____

_____

_____

_____

_____

_____

My favorite thing that happened today:

_____

_____

_____

_____

_____

_____

Today, I feel...

Date: _____

Today I am grateful for...

_____

_____

_____

_____

_____

_____

_____

_____

My favorite thing that happened today:

_____

_____

_____

_____

_____

_____

Today, I feel...

Date: _____

Today I am grateful for...

_____

_____

_____

_____

_____

_____

_____

My favorite thing that happened today:

_____

_____

_____

_____

_____

_____

Today, I feel...

Date: _____

Today I am grateful for...

_____
_____
_____
_____
_____
_____
_____
_____

My favorite thing that happened today:

_____
_____
_____
_____
_____
_____
_____

Today, I feel...

Date: _____

Today I am grateful for...

_____

_____

_____

_____

_____

_____

_____

My favorite thing that happened today:

_____

_____

_____

_____

_____

_____

Today, I feel...

Date: _____

Today I am grateful for...

_____

_____

_____

_____

_____

_____

_____

My favorite thing that happened today:

_____

_____

_____

_____

_____

_____

Today, I feel...

Date: _____

Today I am grateful for...

_____

_____

_____

_____

_____

_____

_____

_____

My favorite thing that happened today:

_____

_____

_____

_____

_____

_____

Today, I feel...

Date: _____

Today I am grateful for...

_____
_____
_____
_____
_____
_____
_____
_____

My favorite thing that happened today:

_____
_____
_____
_____
_____
_____
_____

Today, I feel...

Date: _____

Today I am grateful for...

_____
_____
_____
_____
_____
_____
_____

My favorite thing that happened today:

_____
_____
_____
_____
_____
_____
_____

Today, I feel...

Date: _____

Today I am grateful for...

_____
_____
_____
_____
_____
_____
_____

My favorite thing that happened today:

_____
_____
_____
_____
_____
_____
_____

Today, I feel...

Date: _____

Today I am grateful for...

_____
_____
_____
_____
_____
_____
_____

My favorite thing that happened today:

_____
_____
_____
_____
_____
_____

Today, I feel...

Date: _____

Today I am grateful for...

_____
_____
_____
_____
_____
_____
_____

My favorite thing that happened today:

_____
_____
_____
_____
_____
_____
_____

Today, I feel...

Date: _____

Today I am grateful for...

_____

_____

_____

_____

_____

_____

_____

My favorite thing that happened today:

_____

_____

_____

_____

_____

_____

Today, I feel...

Date: _____

Today I am grateful for...

_____
_____
_____
_____
_____
_____
_____
_____

My favorite thing that happened today:

_____
_____
_____
_____
_____
_____
_____

Today, I feel...

Date: _____

Today I am grateful for...

_____

_____

_____

_____

_____

_____

_____

My favorite thing that happened today:

_____

_____

_____

_____

_____

_____

Today, I feel...

Date: _____

Today I am grateful for...

_____
_____
_____
_____
_____
_____
_____

My favorite thing that happened today:

_____
_____
_____
_____
_____
_____

Today, I feel...

Date: _____

Today I am grateful for...

_____
_____
_____
_____
_____
_____
_____

My favorite thing that happened today:

_____
_____
_____
_____
_____
_____

Today, I feel...

Date: _____

Today I am grateful for...

_____
_____
_____
_____
_____
_____
_____
_____

My favorite thing that happened today:

_____
_____
_____
_____
_____
_____
_____

Today, I feel...

Date: _____

Today I am grateful for...

_____

_____

_____

_____

_____

_____

_____

My favorite thing that happened today:

_____

_____

_____

_____

_____

_____

Today, I feel...

Date: _____

Today I am grateful for...

_____
_____
_____
_____
_____
_____
_____

My favorite thing that happened today:

_____
_____
_____
_____
_____
_____

Today, I feel...

Date: _____

Today I am grateful for...

_____
_____
_____
_____
_____
_____
_____

My favorite thing that happened today:

_____
_____
_____
_____
_____
_____

Today, I feel...

Date: _____

Today I am grateful for...

_____
_____
_____
_____
_____
_____
_____

My favorite thing that happened today:

_____
_____
_____
_____
_____
_____

Today, I feel...

Made in the USA
San Bernardino, CA
15 May 2019